Jack Frost:
Tales Across an Eastern Winter

poems by

Amanda Wochele

Finishing Line Press
Georgetown, Kentucky

Jack Frost:
Tales Across an Eastern Winter

ACKNOWLEDGMENTS

"Jack of Fables" appeared underneath a different name in *Inwood Indiana: Harvest Time*, 2012
"Jack in Armor" appeared underneath a different name in *A cappella Zoo* Issue 8: Spring 2012
"Jack b' Nimble" (Jack b' Slick) appeared in *Black Lantern Publishing*, 2012

Thank you to my family for being my first customers and to Deanna O'Hanna for lending this project your creative eye. Thanks to Finishing Line Press for making my goal a reality.

Publisher: Leah Maines

Editor: Christen Kincaid

Cover Art: Deanna O'Hanna

Author Photo: Deanna O'Hanna, http://www.deannadoes.com/

Cover Design: Elizabeth Maines

Printed in the USA on acid-free paper.
Order online: www.finishinglinepress.com
also available on amazon.com

Author inquiries and mail orders:
Finishing Line Press
P. O. Box 1626
Georgetown, Kentucky 40324
U. S. A.

Table of Contents

To my friends
from Philadelphia

Jack of Fables

He hung upon a crook in the moon
spelling eternity with
shards of ice, but the fall was
hard and he was unable to keep
dawn from breaking. The
next night he ripped the webbing
of a dream catcher showing
desperation in five clawed fingers,
vowing to obliterate every mean,
every deviation keeping him
away. His neck stiffened,
waiting for a star, but
he must have blinked, lacking
discipline. He wished instead on
the taillights of an airplane winking
at him from above, suggestive of a
path. He followed until a bad leg swooned,
then made love to mirages in
the desert while his armor melted
into dust. Stroking a burning sun
He wished of you,
wished of you,
wished of you.
He returned home,
tearing out his hair to spin
into a rope to fling outside
the window in case the door
should jam.

Jack o' the Green
For the Trailblazers

Jack walks down east fourteenth
with his hair grown long cause it
makes him feel older, wearing his
beard like a wreath, he sits down at
the bar with ease, simply saying,
I'll take a beer, and shaking away
the icicles. Bartender, for as old
and Irish that he is, knows every
trick that's played on him: knows
the kid, by face and name, and
knows he's got no business being
here. But it's the day before and
the streets look clear and he might
be in the wrong here, but by the
red in Jack's eye, and the green
of his face, he'd swear the season's
been a longer one.

He pours two beers and tops
them off—*I hope I'm not
overstepping my boundaries here*-
leaning across the bar to offer the
worldly advice before the kid's
up and done with it—*but I seen
the worst o' every town that flanks
the wide Atlantic, seen baby Jesus
crested in the face of every east-ta-
westerner, and—well, fuck, if
there's anything I know best, it's:*

*Happiness comes easiest to the
ones who don't care about it,
realize it, or think about it, to
those who've never fought a day
in their life for it...*

for instance:

some crank three rounds out of
an M1 carbine and get a hard on,
and some never get over it, the
cold-sweat of heaving soviets
across the eastern front and the
yanks swelling the western bend—
here, Jack's grandfather
became a veteran, escaping death
by the nines, freed in the burst of
springtime yet it's December he
remembers—how trills of bells
that Christmas day banged through
his head for all eternity!—echoing
through silver fir in all its frigid
filigree, shedding crystal quills
to fill the gash where splashed in
the red the brains would be, across
those pristine dress greens of his
shrieking, marching enemy: *Möge
Gott reinigen ihren Chaos!*
(may God clean your mess, bitch)
cocking a rifle against his head
before retreating, knowing there
were no drycleaners hidden in the
thick, green forest.

He took hatchet to the brush
and cut his way out of it—nine
years post millennial he will watch
Jack graduate, but then, in the
bleached-out flush of dawn, he
knew what it was he'd pass along:

that the day drags on as long as
night; that there's truth to your
demons in the stark, blonde light.

His mother arrived spun from
cold air and built for survival: ready
on the right, with bones fleshed
from the Rhine, ready on the left,
where she tiptoed along a reef of
the Delaware, babbling brags about
a battle of the bold—*you see, yours
is not the first war I've lived
through!*—grown up in a plot of
Chester, but there he could have
grown up anywhere...

*...close your eyes, feel the wind
catch your hair as it breathes
a new city into you, suddenly
there's life in you...*

but even at his best he'll never
match that crisp flag stabbed in
the ground, and when his nerves
are getting the best of him again,
she'll swear it's the German
pounding through his veins that's
baiting the madness in him.

Outside, Jack mistakes the swirl
of snow for ghosts, hanging the
sky in gray, ramming the rightfully-
remaining day with the night

they've brought along. He shakes
his head, pats his face, and asks
for something stronger, something
warmer, but bartender warns him,
swearing:

(Young man) *We are the great
artificers! We make our whiskey like
we build our ships: absolutely fuckin'
drownable, drink the stuff just to
watch it piss right out o' ya.*

He presses the glass in front of
Jack and clears away the rest: *I
hope you're one who can handle it.*

Jack's fucked up, praying the old
man would just shut up already
hearing only the *blah blah blah* of
him, *cut your hair, why don't ya,*
his mouth rolling around the way
trout gulp for air, and then: *if you've
ever seen the way blood drains
from a body ya'd put up more of
a fight,* sounds a lot like spite, don't
it? spilling over god's good earth,
the red blended deep against the
green, a prick of the vine and
the king has come clean—but it
was not what He intended.

Jack b' Nimble (Jack b' Slick)

Jack be a son-of-a bitch, tilting his
head to let sun light his cigarette-stick,
but at night he's known to use anything
from streetlamps to lanterns; the left of
his face crumpled with his head in a
blue-lit stovetop, which made the police
report difficult.

The day he left his girl looked
exhausted: "his stride made a walk
in the park undoable, but our passion—
unmatchable," feeling the stretch
in his limbs and ribs through the skin
that glowed in the dark.

The gas station clerk claimed Jack
had a thirst for the stuff, but when asked
why he failed to report strange behavior he
shrugged, saying: "the kid had a
foot out the door before I could count
his change."

He was the last to see Jack.

His girlfriend was in a state of
undone, waiting for the backwards
glance of a one-eyed stare
until news came—

"We've lost Jack
   to wantonness," said the officer,
"the way a cowboy rides straight into
the setting sun and is burned
to bits." When she demanded evidence,
they brought back the heap of ashes:
the muscle gone,
and the skin all gone,
but all his bones are lit.

Jack in Armor

I. Artemis Corona

In heavy crowd by early night,
men knot ties tight to the neck and
loosen bands of their belts, forgetting
they have babies or have had them.
Buy Baby a round, babe; see them growing
sickly like stars dripping
off an 8-ball, spying
on waitresses.
Queer, she thinks, of what brings him
to his knees: the Virgin, to peer
up Her robes—
virgin! She who makes love only to Moon:
Strawberry, Harvest, Hunter's:
hers, a lazy bloom, but sanguine just the
same—
She spills sangria in chalices
carried above the crown:

Concentrate, try again.

The fruit falls,
soaking down her front thigh.
If Scorpion's the season
she'll wince at the pinch when a hand
slides under, four fingers
straddled down the middle, the index free
to flick. Straight down the middle,
Lidge had done it that year, when they said it was
devastating they were talking
about the release.

II. Canis Minor

Old man sits earthbound, slowing
time while bartender
muddles cherry into his glass.
Dry summer in the north village,
an exotic spirit gave him dysentery:
Go home, Old Man.
Sixty-one years, my father wore
shirt and tie that day they lost
to the Yanks, he was once
handsome like you.

A pat, a grin, prick o' a pin then
off to 'Nam he bade me—
(Go home, old man!)—In swampy
morgue the boys wore George and
laughed at my little golden lady.

Jeanne D'Arc, sa petite fille—
Jeanne D'Arc, son amant à Philadelphie!

Old Man, go home.

He wore shirt and tie that day,
hell I never seen him look so sad either.

III. Orion's Belt

Mayberry bats live, alive, the black
of him blotting lights in HD
he reaches a hand down and scratches
gemstones between his legs.
"Don't let me down," then tug
their flies the moment he straddles
the plate, berated palms
wrapped tight around the bat.

There he goes—Mayberry
spread-legged with his right
shoulder pulled up and bulging bright
in the night—the men howl:
don't let me down—
The edifice of his shoulders! The steeple of his jaw!
Skywards towards Saints who flank
the Bank.
Men cry out
in sluttish surrender because
there's a sort of relief when
heart releases ethanol in
perfect balmy breaths.

IV. Betelgeuse

Attaboy! Attaboy! shots for all, he says,
walk in my bar like you'd walk in Pete's
Cathedral, he says. Never know
which alchemist pisses in whiskey
with lights so low. Bastard knows
it's transfers of momentum and velocity
and little air resistance—
then, a victory is decidedly so.
He's seen boys run all
the plates, seen ones burnt
after third, debased at
the last forty after
ninety-ninety-ninety balking
blindly at the home free. Seen enough
to hold the muddler off the palm
and into the fingers but
he's never seen this.

He climbs into a choke,
his heavy pour fingering psalms
out of voices of men.
Outside a chill stings
in tiny barbs. In this direction,
night falters; it shrinks upon
a scattering of stars burning to
death while they wait.

He's got Johnny by the neck
and another on the stem until they've
sworn the trinity with the steady hand
because moonlight won't
stain the glass until next morning.

Jack's Diamonds
(New York City: February, 2012)

Jack sleeps on the fifth pier by the river, below a batch
of buildings he stares at nightly like a stacked rack,
counting each spire by the karat until provoked by
lack of symmetry, waking pissed off and shivering,
he fights a familiar sense of misery as he chokes on cold air,
chugging it like a draught beer til' suddenly its "fuck the
Patriots before 9/11, and fuck 'em after," cause it takes more
than one disaster when aiming any higher than an
empire.

They who agree toss coins to see Jack blast down Atlantic
like a 40-yard-line, caring more for the play
than he gives a shit for dinner, whipping past the corner for a
quarter-pounder, pumping heat through holes in the soles
of his sneakers and smoking the pavement like a laser
beam.

He looks for a bench to rest once reaching the terminal
streets, barely able to catch his breath when what yesterday
was a heap of splinters is now shielded in weathered
corten steel, engineered to wrap a crowd of 20,000 within an
unfinished billion that keels his knees onto the cold-hard
ground as he watches the new indoor facility promise, in
cool neon blue sincerity, to sweat the brows of athletes passing
through an eastern winter next year.

Here, he hangs around for the last Hail Mary, following a path
of cheers singing Eli, Eli, Eli, whiplashed by the guy
who just might prove God's a tank of a white dude, laughing
from the sidelines, daring every last one of these motherfuckers
to shoot down the 219 pounds of southern hospitality jackin' up
his salary by the goal line, offering the casualties to a
cold-weather city basking in the overcast.

Tonight, every karat in the spire beams like sapphires,
and it's hard to see if that sheet of ice across the east river
is a trick of the streetlights or the glint of unpolished
diamonds. Though this season in particular has been one of the
mildest, the blue light cutting a perpendicular will remind them
to be generous, and he'll stand another night without falling,
roaming the avenue for a hand to shake, a bet to make, not
knowing how bitchin' cold the wind will be
blowing across the meadowlands next winter.

Jack Slays

every beast hidden underneath the bed,
the best in the area, he's never scared,
catching and tossing monsters into the
night sky—see! they scramble away
like *butterflies*.

He's even checked below the
piano, careful not to hit his head:
he's a big kid who doesn't get caught
out of position, doesn't mind the cold
winds creeping in, in fact—he only
sweats it away:

there's always a plan playing in his
head for the savages who crawl out
from under him just to squint at his
shadow, for the maniacs who spaz
out, frozen at the sight of him—

the witnesses are unsure of how far
down he slashed the ice this time, but
they do know a few winters will pass
before the tears disappear—
and all of this, they know, he does
on holy ground,

sparing the innocent.

He claims he appreciates the game
too much to see the end of it, to mind
the pressure of it—getting blasted by
heat, then, flexed and ready, he pulls
it off again—cooler,
fresher.

Jack @ the Top of the Beanstalk

Jack grew up the son of a
bridge painter out of Union
City, learning young how high
it feels to live life within the
crux of the lifted sun. Way up
here, he's seen how light
bends against tempered
glass, fracturing shards of
warmth into dents of silver
& gold in the depths of a new-
year's winter—

they come in from all over,
standing in coats on the
plaza below, taking photos
of it, but whichever way they
filter it won't capture the exact
flash that strips the light of
the sun off the white of the
snow—but eventually he
comes down from it,
touching ground zero when
the glass of his eyes
flood over,

look:

there is a point out there on
the Hudson from which it is
impossible to look away
from; a tiny dot frosted across
the buried blue blur of the lost,
son: if there's anything to
take away from this it's that
illusions bridge what's
faraway;

bone white is the snow the
morning after a good lay,
heavy heaving snow, lying
awake and breathing still, yet
they told him stay home,
de Blasio having the balls to
say the coast took a *pounding*,
but which politician really
knows how badly impact
hurts—

and who knows Brooklyn
is the coldest place on Earth—
somewhere to sit comatose in
the tub while he shreds his
brain to pieces, heat chilling
skin that's already cold as a
voodoo voice on the subway
delivers the blow: *loosen
up, crybaby—Saddam
Hussein cannot go to hell
for people like you.*

Smoke twists his room in a
slow-moving binge, seeping
into his limbs, staining through
the ceiling, and he can't help
in feeling a little romantic,
thinking flesh might grow
back where its planted, so
when he pries up a window
he doesn't even realize the
things which lie beneath him
are freezing.

It's only through the haze

when he finally sees it: that
ghosts float out on puffs of
a cloud, and those sounds
were just blown around by
the wind. Jack sort of laughs,
extending the stem of his
neck out into the thick of the
draft, breathing in until the
lump in his throat relaxes,
because no, he knows,
he won't get any higher
than this.

Jack Frost

Jack was around to see the first black president, and
when the east turned blue they buckled down, running
toward the deep months hand in hand, only a little
black and blue

if nothing else, at least he can tell his children this, so
they may see what the sun is capable of though it won't
always shine directly on their faces -

these states are such homeless places; he's not totally
sure who belongs with who anymore,

and he can't recall where he left his measuring cup the
last time he changed cities, but the broom is always
behind the desk.

he wishes the Atlantic could crest more gently, if only
he could see through and into the bottom,

then,

there'd be reason to ramble at its edge again, because
he is someone who's loved every living thing

that's passed through his arms and now the gasp
between the right and the left feels a bit like drowning
could be.

at night,
and in mornings,

of course it gets cold, but the open air against the
breadth of his chest hits him differently

every time.

Jack of All

In the weeks preceding the accident,
Jack was in a constant state of vexation,
blasting down Route 1 on two wheels,
the strangest was he wouldn't go any place
with yellow walls anymore,
a repercussion of him never having cried
as an infant—only cursed up a storm
in his crib.

His parents remember how they painted
in white up to the ceiling,
in a room crisp as snow, they prayed
for ten fingers and ten toes—he never was
a cozy kid, had trouble backing off the
clutch, never fit in the way others did,
only loved to shift up and jerk them
around.

Death was the place he visited when
he wore the road out flat: it was a
big, clear space with beveled edges, he
found it on a strip of asphalt behind PHL,
his Fury destroyed on the ground, his
left leg split like an axe to a rotted tree,
and when takeoff delayed he cried out
once, in a noise that didn't even sound
like crying.

He imagined it would've taken all of him,
as a whole body fits into a hole, never
guessed it was so metonymic, the
limb a spit out-and- severed parting gift
before the flight took off: he knows now
those revved-up races on 95, the airless
spaces on the Verrazano—what does it
fucking matter? If he's not dead yet, then
he's passed on in other places and
he's not too sure what it was he
expected:

That god is real? Yes,
and still with him, waiting at O'Hare:
the carpets, the tiles, at least, are
always going to be there.

(for our lost friends)

Jack of Ever After   or,   The Jack of Hearts

They've said Jack never buries the dead, but raises them,
so when word spread they crawled out of every corner,
bearing to him their lists of names:

it happened once, on the season's first fall of rain,
then quickly came the morning light, bouncing off
bones in the faces of those they've missed.

feel me in the morning air feel me, feel me, feel me
there.

In the handful of debris he pried off Orion he showed
them a man redeemed, saying his goodbyes to the night
sky in a sound that could only be something of nostalgia,
biting off slabs of his youth for the hungry to swallow
whole, 'cause he has *never been afraid to die*—is what he
told them.

There are other lives to live, *and if I can't get by in*
this one, I know I'll try harder on my next run. All
his life he's made mistakes, and every time a star blows
he's bound toward another.

Born across a spring equinox, he feels the bulk of dark
brawled against light, knows a dead man walks the earth
above not without consequence, the heavy of the dirt
rolled across the valley green and yet the sky overhead
must bear all this—

and yet, and yet, and yet—
he's worth that weight in solid gold.

Amanda Wochele grew up in Woodlyn, Pennsylvania. At ten years old, her short story "Shamu's Big Adventure" won a Young Author's Award in Delaware County, and she has been writing ever since. Upon graduating Ridley High School in 2009, her short story "On Myth and Mortality" was published in *The Wordstock Ten*. She then received a Bachelor of Arts in English and Literature from Temple University in Philadelphia, PA, while publishing poetry in *A Capella Zoo, Inwood Indiana, Black Lantern Press,* and *The Write to Read: Response Journals that Increase Comprehension*. Most recently, her poem, "Climate Control" appeared in *Whirlwind #9*, (2016).

In 2013, Amanda moved to Brooklyn, New York to obtain her Masters of Arts in American literature from Brooklyn College, writing her thesis under the counsel of graduate deputy and author Dr. James Davis. Her thesis, entitled "A Heap of Broken Images: The Undead in William Faulkner's *As I Lay Dying*," provided a structural study of the novel within the horror genre. Her essay detailing Irish folk literature was among the chosen few to be presented at the Seventh Annual Brooklyn College Graduate English Conference in 2014.

Amanda has since moved back to Philadelphia and continues writing. Her first chapbook, *Jack: Tales Across an Eastern Winter,* is inspired by the people of these two great east coast cities. She is thrilled to present her work to the public.

www.ingramcontent.com/pod-product-compliance
Lightning Source LLC
LaVergne TN
LVHW021127080426
835510LV00021B/3349